The Yoko Ono

Broken Jaw Press
Box 596 Stn A   **www.brokenjaw.com**
Fredericton NB E3B 5A6   jblades@nbnet.nb.ca
Canada   tel / fax 506 454-5127

Velvet Touch 4
Velvet Touch series editor: R.M. Vaughan

Cover: production photo — Lee Pui Ming as Yoko. Photo by Heather Morton.
Author photo by Tim Leyes
Proofreading by Sue McCluskey
Design and in-house editing by the publisher, Joe Blades
Printed and bound in Canada by Sentinel Printing, Yarmouth NS

Second printing: March 2003

The Yoko Ono Project was previously published by PUC Play Service, Playwrights Union of Canada, Toronto, January 2000, ISBN 1-55173-660-8.

The publisher gratefully acknowledges the support of the Canada Council for the Arts and the New Brunswick Department of Education, Culture and Sport Secretariat-Arts Development Branch.

National Library of Canada Cataloguing in Publication Data
Yoon, Jean, 1962-
        The Yoko Ono project / by Jean Yoon ; with instruction poems,
music, and other texts by Yoko Ono.

(Velvet touch ; 4)
A play.
Includes bibliographical references.
ISBN 1-55391-001-X

        1. Ono, Yoko—Drama. I. Ono, Yoko II. Title. III. Series: Velvet touch (Fredericton, N.B.) ; 4.

PS8597.O4Y64 2002   C812'.54   C2002-903765-4
PR9199.3.Y48Y65 2002

The Yoko Ono Project

by Jean Yoon

with
Instruction Poems, Music, and Other Texts
by Yoko Ono

Fredericton • Canada

"All my work is a form of wishing."
"I thought art was a verb rather than a noun"
— Yoko Ono

Production History

The Yoko Ono Project was first workshopped at Nightwood Theatre's Groundswell Festival, Toronto. It was presented in a public reading in March 1995 at the Theatre Centre West, Toronto, directed by Sarah Stanley and featuring the following actors:

Tammy	Jane Luk
Jo	M.J. Kang
Helen	Denise Fujiwara
David/John	Bruce Beaton

A longer version was workshopped at the Banff Playwrights' Colony, Banff, Alberta in 1995 with Kim McCaw, Artistic Director.

A much revised draft underwent an intensive two week multimedia workshop, produced by Loud Mouth Asian Babes, and culminated in a one night 'Concert Reading' as part of Under the Umbrella, at Theatre Centre East, Toronto, on 28 January 1996 with the following artists:

Helen	Quyen Hua
Jo	M.J. Kang
Tammy	Susan Lee
Maureen	Valerie Sing Turner
David/John	Bruce Beaton
Singer/Yoko	Sook-Yin Lee

Director	Sarah Stanley
Composer	Lee Pui Ming
Set Design	Troy Hansen
Media Design	Helen Lee
Assistant Director	Soraya Peerbaye

Stage Manager Ruthe Whiston

Technician   T.J. Shamata

Administrator   Diane Laundy

The Yoko Ono Project premiered January 13, 2000 at Theatre Passe Muraille, Toronto — produced by Theatre Passe Muraille and Loud Mouth Asian Babes.

Helen   Denise Fujiwara

Jo   M.J. Kang

Tammy   Keira Loughran

David/John   Bruce Beaton

Gus   Glenn Marc Silot

Singer/Yoko   Lee Pui Ming

Directors   Jean Yoon and Marion de Vries

Dramaturges   Marion de Vries and Iris Turcott

Set Design   Vikki Anderson

Lighting Design   Bonnie Beecher

Original Music   Lee Pui Ming

Sound Design   Jonathan Rooke

Choreography   Eryn Dace Trudell

Costume Design   Joanne LeBlanc

Media Design   Chris Clifford

Media Materials Coordinator and Video Installation Director
                    Jennifer Yap

Stage Manager   Tanya Greve

Assistant Stage Manager

                    Claire Adams

Production Manager

                    Mark Ryder

Co-Producer for LMAB and Studio One Liaison

Valerie Sing Turner

The Yoko Ono Project received its West Coast premiere at The Firehall Arts Centre in Vancouver on 17 November 2001 with the following artists:

Helen	Donna Yamamoto
Jo	Laara Ong
Tammy	Adrienne Wong
David/John	Peter Grier
Gus	Daniel Chen
Singer/Yoko	Maiko Bae Yamamoto

Director	Donna Spencer
Set Design	Omanie Elias
Lighting Design	James Proudfoot
Sound/Musical Direction	
	Noah Drew
Slides/Video:	Tim Matheson
Costume Design	Barbara Clayden

Playwright's Acknowledgments

I am grateful to Nightwood Theatre, the Banff Playwrights Colony, and the whole Theatre Passe Muraille clan — Jacoba Knappen, Layne Coleman, Taylor Rath and David Kinsman. I am deeply indebted to everyone who has contributed to the development of the piece: Iris Turcott who emphatically reminded me of my first impulses in writing this piece; Marion de Vries for incisive, vigilant and inspiring dramaturgy, directorial vision, and true friendship; Valerie Sing Turner for invaluable support and hard, hard work; Lee Pui Ming, Eryn Dace Trudell, Vikki Anderson, Jennifer Yap, Joanne LeBlanc, M.J. Kang, Denise Fujiwara, Bruce Beaton, Keira Loughran, Glenn Marc Silot, Jane Luk, Chris Clifford, Mark Ryder, Tanya Greve, Claire Adams, Bonnie Beecher, Jonathan Rooke, Roger West, Bill Stahl, Susan Lee, Sook-Yin Lee, Sarah Stanley, Troy Hansen; Quyen Hua, Ruthe Whiston and all the artists who contributed to the piece.

Thank you also to Kishwar Iqbal, maxine bailey, Alan Williams, Koto Sato, Kim McCaw, Robert Allen, Kwoi Gin, Wayson Choy, all my friends at T.A.P.E.; Stephen Wiggins and Dr. Chow for letting me write at the farm; Joanne Peterson, Kevin Concannon, Marsha Ewing, and all my fellow ONOnetters who shared information and materials on Ono; Algo MacNada, Pat Galbraith, Michael Hollett, Ben Kim and other friends who passed on precious Ono materials. Merci, to Richard Joly for his dedication to all things Ono! Gratitude to Karla Merrifield, Michael Philips, all the staff of Studio One; to Sam Havadtoy and to the one and only Yoko Ono whose work inspired the show and whose generosity allowed for us to reproduce her work in the production.

The Yoko Ono Project was written with the financial assistance and generous support of The Canada Council for the Arts, the Ontario Arts Council Playwright Recommender Program, the Laidlaw Foundation, the Toronto Arts Council and my parents, Taek-Soon and Chung-Bin Yoon who fed me when I was destitute.

Preface

I envision this piece as a multimedia presentation, a theatrical reflection of Ono's obsession with the bare image, her fluid movement from one medium to another, and her consistent focus on breaking one's expectations of what art is and where its borders lie.

A musician provides the spine of sound which is augmented by a soundscape of Ono's music, excerpts from taped interviews and other archival material.

The Characters

Helen	Inquiring, questioning. High-strung.
Jo	Sensual, sly, subversive, rebellious. An artist who uses her wit as a weapon.
Tammy	Young, naive. In love with David, torn by choices. A peacemaker.
Singer/Yoko	Performance artist, singer, landscape figure, part of Yoko's Box.
David	Tammy's boyfriend. Twenties. Decent, nice, a good guy. White.
Gus	Helen's brother. 20s. Goofy, awkward, a fine core of anger.
Idiot Man	May be played be either David or Gus.

Note:

Where material by Yoko Ono is performed by anyone other than the Singer/Yoko, the performer is indicated as Jo Yoko or Helen Yoko and so on ...

Playwright's Note:

The Yoko Ono Project is inspired by Yoko Ono's work and music and life; and the engine of the play, the central theatrical premise, is an Ono piece entitled "Part Painting". Essentially a letter, accompanied by a 3 inch by 3 inch square of blank white paper, a single portion.

The text of "Part Painting" begins much as our version of "Part Painting" does, congratulating the recipient, inviting him/her to a future event to 'put all the pieces together and appreciate the painting in its original form'. The letter then goes on to inquire about friends and neighbours who might also enjoy receiving a portion of "Part Painting" and requesting detailed information, address, occupation, annual income, 'to determine how large a section' of "Part Painting" they should receive.

Created in the early '60s, "Part Painting" is a mischievous investigation of our notions of art as object, its fickle value in the marketplace and is, essentially, a send-up of direct marketing. More importantly "Part Painting" reprises a number of themes in Ono's Fluxus era work: the notions of gathering, reassembling a fractured object, the whimsical notion of an ideal, an 'original form', the insistence on the imagination as the realm in which art lives and is created.

The Yoko Ono Project is itself a gathering, an effort to reconstitute a fractured understanding of Ono, her work, and of ourselves. The characters and audience are brought to the theatre/gallery by "Part Painting". Anyone entering the theatre *must* receive a portion of *Part Painting*, a simple 3" x 3" square of blank white paper.

As part of the event, it would be ideal too if, in the lobby, there were a "Wishing Tree" on which audience members can tie a ribbon or perhaps attach their portion of "Part Painting" after the show, making a wish and completing the circle.

The Stage

A bare stage suggesting an art gallery. White, squarish, the theatre presents itself as a box, an empty box, Yoko's Box. On the stage are three empty exhibit stands. Also a large and mysterious box, "The Danger Box", off to the side. In the original production the "Danger Box" was constructed from opaque two-way mirror, so that it reflected light but was transparent when lit from within. Throughout the production, as during during the "Part Painting" scenes, screens on which images can be projected fall and unfurl.

The Yoko Ono Project

Scene 1:   Part Painting[1]

Music: "Part Painting Theme".

Sound: (Tape loop.) "Yoko's Box"

Jo, wearing sunglasses, marches on stage holding a small square of paper. She looks at it curiously. Turns it over. It is blank.

Singer/Yoko: Congratulations! You are one of 10,000 selected individuals to whom we have sent this "Part Painting" by Yoko Ono.

Helen walks on stage, puzzled by what she sees — a small square of paper. She turns it over and examines it intently.

Singer/Yoko: Each person has received a portion of this painting. On *(Date of performance.)* we are holding a gathering to put all the parts together and appreciate the painting in its original form.

Tammy is propelled on stage. Is she late? She carries a piece of paper. She takes her place. She is nervous.

Singer/Yoko: The gathering — which we will call "The Yoko Ono Project" — will begin — now.

Sound: Ting of Wishing Bell.

The women look at each other and then look at the pieces of paper. They look out at the audience. They resemble deer in traffic headlights. Action stops. Blackout.

Scene 2: Lighting Piece[2]

Slide: *"Lighting Piece"*

Four Yokos light matches, stare into them, watching them burn. Four Yokos acknowledge the audience. They are very still and nervous. They each hold their match out to the audience so they can see it burn.

Slide: *"Light a match and watch till it goes out." (y.o. 1955)*

All Yokos: I ... uh, I ... am, uh, very .... Shhhh ....

The Yokos smile apologetically at the audience. They each hold out their match and watch it burn. Darkness.

Scene 3: Falling Piece

Slide: *"Falling Piece", (y.o., 1964 spring)*

Video: Tammy, Helen and Jo appear dimly lit as a video image of the three of them, together or separately, is projected so that the effect is of disembodiment, alienation, double-vision. A cool and seductive voice from the darkness reads lines underlined.

Singer/Yoko: Go outside of you.
　　　　　　Look at yourself walking down the street.
　　　　　　Make yourself tumble on a stone and fall.
　　　　　　Watch it.
　　　　　　Watch other people looking.
　　　　　　Observe carefully how you fall.[3]

Video: Tammy trips, stumbles; Jo plummets as from a very high, high place. Helen staggers, struggles, remains standing, as if unfinished.

Scene 4:   **Helen Falling ...**

Idiot Man: Hey, Yoko! Yoko Ono!

Helen: It happens. All the time. When you least expect it. On your way home from the corner store. Walking alone. Late at night. There's just you. Walking. You are happy, content, strong, throwing all your worries out into the world, off of your shoulders, shimmying it off of your body like a snake shedding its skin. You're calming, coming down from a hard day, a long week, coming down like a kite skimming back to earth. You're listening to the rhythm of your footsteps, your breathing and all of sudden you feel a car braking behind you, you don't see it you feel it, the aggressive thrust of its wheels, braking too hard, too fast —

Idiot Man: Hey Yoko! Yoko ONO!

Helen: You turn, you turn, and then you see him. He's just a guy, your age, maybe older, you can't tell, his arm's swinging out of the passenger window, pointing at you. And he's laughing, his mouth is moving, he's saying things ...

Idiot Man: HEY, YOKO BABY, WANNA —

Helen: *(Charging.)* YOU FUCKING FUCK! FUCK YOU! YOU THINK THAT'S FUCKIN' FUNNY, YOU YOU YOU —

Sound: Laughter. Screeching of car going off.

Helen stunned and alone. Helen weeps, chokes, has trouble breathing. Lights down on Helen crying.

Scene 5:   **Breathe**[4]

Slide: Breathe

Jo Yoko: I must have been about eight or nine when I
               started ... breathing. Very quietly. Very still. I
               was a serious child. I was a frightened child. I
               was afraid that if I didn't count my breathings, if
               I didn't pay attention that perhaps I would
               forget. *(She breathes several times.)* If I don't
               count them, would I not breathe? Would I?[5]

She watches the audience nervously, breathing ...

Scene 6:   **Snapshots**

*Slide: Fade up on photo images of Yoko Ono in the late
'60s - early '70s, with sunglasses and long hair.*

Three women enter. Jo wearing sunglasses.

Helen: I don't wear sunglasses. I rarely wear my hair
               down and only with friends, only when I feel
               comfortable. You know that phrase 'to let your
               hair down'? It's not a metaphor with me. I
               never do the two at once — wear sunglasses
               and my hair down at the same time. Never.
               Otherwise it's stupid comments like:

Man: "You know, you look just like Yoko Ono."

Helen: Gee, thanks.

Tammy: I, ah, just wanna say, ah, I think, I think Yoko
               Ono is, is really cool. She's ... *awesome*. And I
               think this is, this is *important*. But I just ah ....
               She's just not a life threatening issue for me, I
               just wanted to say that.

Slide: Image of Yoko circa 1966, the young artist.

Jo: You know when Yoko Ono first hit the London
        art scene in the early sixties the headline was
        'Yoko Ono High Priestess of the Happening'[6].
        She was way ahead of her time, doing these far
        out things that really shook people up, making
        them think about what art is. She's a major
        inspiration for me as an artist. Major.

Helen: It started when I was a teenager, seventeen,
        eighteen. I didn't even know who Yoko Ono
        was then. I knew who the Beatles were but I
        didn't know much about them. I didn't know
        who John Lennon was, exactly, and I didn't
        know that Yoko Ono was married to him. I
        didn't care! She is just a name to me, Yoko Ono,
        a thing people say to me because I am Asian.

Slide: Image of Yoko now, and/or cover of Rising[7]

Tammy: I also have her new album, *Rising*. It was a
        present from, well, my boyfriend.

Jo: She is one of a kind. Like John Lennon said, the
        most famous undiscovered artist in the world.

Helen: I don't look at all like her.

Tammy: He's supposed to be here, actually. You haven't,
        like, seen him, have you? Leather jacket. Hair to
        about here? My boyfriend, the one who gave me
        Rising. He's really into her ...

Helen: So why do people keep going on about it? Why
        do they say it with that awful look in their eyes?
        Yoko Ono ...

Tammy: Yoko Ono.

Jo: Yoko Ono ... *(Takes centre stage.)* Picture this:
        I'm eighteen. A little more plump. Messy hair.
        Longer. Naive. Eager. I'm living on my own in
        downtown Toronto. And I'm determined to lose
        my virginity, my innocence and anything else I

can leave behind. My history maybe. I hang out in bars and cafes wearing all black antique clothing. Vintage items that I find at garage sales. I learn to smoke. Drink. I get a boyfriend. He's attractive ... to me.... There are no obvious signs of deviancy.

The first time we make love we're at his place. We're necking, undressing each other. I like the way he kisses. Soft and wet. Gentle.... He puts on some music.

Music: *Starts in softly. "Hard Days Night"[8].*

Jo: It's nice. We're touching, exploring.... Skin skin so much skin and muscle and sweat. I feel ... mmmmmmm ... and the music is going ...

Music: *Music goes loud.*

Jo: and I'm warm all over like melting caramel ...

Sound: *Woman breathing, fast, faster ...*

Rehearsal photo — M.J. Kang as Jo.   Photo by Yeung-Seu Yoon

Jo:	And he's getting closer and closer and harder and faster andandand suddenly his head snaps up, he arches back like a swimmer gasping for air and he screams, he moans, he cries —
Guy:	Oh, oh, OHHHH, yokoyoko YOKOYOOOKOOOOO!
Music/Sound:	*Stop. Beat.*
Jo:	And that was the end of that. It's a true story. More or less.

Scene 7: Truth/False[9]

Slide: Truth/False

Helen Yoko:	True or False. Please answer the following questions true or false. Thank you.

Mt. Fuji, whose color is blue and white from the distance and volcano red when you go near, is a carefully planned modern Japanese project built to attract tourists.

Grapefruit is a hybrid of lemon and orange.

Snow is a hybrid of wish and lament.

Teeth and bones are solid forms of cloud.

There is a transparent peace tower in New York City which casts no shadow and, therefore, is very rarely recognized.

What is a circle event?

Helen Yoko waits, watches. Gus walks on, clutching a piece of "Part Painting". He circles, lost, lost, lost. He exits.

Scene 8:   Blood Object

Slide: "Blood Objects"

Slide: Images of Blood Objects – "Mirror", "Hairbrush", and finally "High-Heeled Shoes", 1993.[10] A pair of scary stiletto shoes with blood on the edges.

Jo, Helen and Tammy circle around an exhibit stand, examining the Ono's "Blood Object" works.

Jo: Cool, eh? "Blood Object". It's one of her more recent pieces. Bronze. I love it. It's so simple and creepy. And so clear in its indictment of how women are seduced into the pursuit of power through beauty, how we will exorcize our sexuality and savage our bodies for that extra edge.

Helen: It's horrifying.

Jo: Exactly. Very Japanese in that respect.

Helen exits, disgruntled. David enters, looking for Tammy.

Jo: *(To Tammy)* Hey, Rice King alert. Check this out.

Jo smokes aggressively. David doesn't see Tammy, veers off. Tammy is confused.

Jo: Nothing keeps a Rice King away like a smoking cigarette.

Tammy: Pardon me?

Jo: Rice King. White guy with a fetish for Asian women.

Tammy: I've never heard that before.

Jo: It's useful.

Tammy: But not all white guys are Rice Kings. I mean, I don't think — I mean, I mean, my boyfriend's white but he isn't a ...

Jo: Rice King.

Tammy:	Right. But that doesn't mean there aren't some around. I mean, I think I know the guys you mean ...
Jo:	Jo. Jo-Song.
Tammy:	I'm Tammy. Anyway, uhm, David, he isn't like that.
Jo:	He's your ...
Tammy:	Yeah. I mean, I think so.... He's supposed to be here, actually, my you know ...

Tammy rushes off.

Scene 9:   Closet Piece

Slide: "Closet Piece"

Singer/Yoko: Closet Piece I.

Think of a piece you lost.
Look for it in your closet.

Closet Piece II.

Put one memory into one half of your head.
Shut if off and forget it.
Let the other half of the brain long for it. [11]

Sound: John and Yoko, The Wedding Album[12]. A short audio clip of John and Yoko calling after each other, playful, searching, desperate, comical ...

Scene 10:   Tammy and David

Tammy looks for David but can't find him. Despondent, she slumps, head in hands. David crosses on other side of gallery. Tammy looks up. Once they touch they remain in contact without break.

Tammy: David? David! Hey, David!

David: Tammy!? I've been looking all over for you!

Tammy: Oh, David, I'm so glad you're here. I saw you earlier, you know, walking around, but uhm, you didn't see me, did you?

David: No.

Tammy: This woman was talking about "Rice Kings" in this really, I don't know, judgmental kind of way, you know. And I just felt really weird and kind of, I don't know, scrunched, you know?

David: Tammy, what are you talking about?

Tammy: I don't know, what are you talking about?

David: I asked you first.

Tammy: Well, I asked you second.

David: Did not!

Tammy: Did too.

Tickling match that ends with Tammy's bag falling to the ground. A change of clothes, toiletries, toothbrush etc.

David: Toothbrush, clean clothes ... are you coming over tonight. To stay the night? No sneaking off at two in the morning?

Tammy: Well, I was wondering if maybe ...

David: Maybe? Tammy! Tammy!

Picks her up and hugs her, spins her.

Scene 11:   Gus and Helen at "Danger Box"

Helen is visibly relieved to see Gus.

Gus: Hey Helen, did you see those shoes? Kind of, I
            don't know, kinky, hunh?

Helen: Gus!

Gus: What? I'm a guy! I can't help it. What? What!
            Just because you're my nesan doesn't mean you
            have to be — you're not Neighbourhood Watch,
            okay? Oh man, there are so many good-looking
            women here. Art galleries, that's where it's at. I
            wish someone had *told* me.

Helen: Gus!

Gus: What? Isn't this cool? Aren't you glad you came?

Helen: No, I don't know. I mean, okay, *I* got the
            invitation, but *you're* the one who wanted to
            come. And first thing through the door, you're
            off somewhere.... It's not like when we were
            kids at Disneyland —

Gus: I was seven, Helen, when are you going to let that
            go!

Helen: When you stop dragging me out, oh it'll be great!
            Then dump me just because I'm your sister.
            Christ, what am *I* doing at a *Yoko* event? I don't
            even —

Gus: Whooooaaa!! Whoa, whoa, Helen, don't touch
            that.

Helen: Don't touch what?

Gus: Danger. Danger. It's says *Danger.*

Helen: "Danger Box". It's just a box, Gus. A box.

Gus: "Machine that you will never come back the
            same from if you get in."[13] It's an *idea*, Helen.
            You don't mess with *ideas.*

Scene 12:   Part Painting 2

Slide: "Part Painting 2"

Music: "Part Painting" Theme

Sound: (Tape loop.) "Yoko's Box"

Jo enters now with several small squares of paper. Curious, a little puzzled. Helen enters, also carrying squares of papers, perhaps one in her hair?

Singer/Yoko: Congratulations! You are one of 10,000 selected individuals to whom we have sent this "Part Painting" by Yoko Ono.

David enters, exits. Tammy enters opposite, just misses him.

Singer/Yoko: Each person has received a portion of this painting. On *(Date of performance.)* we are holding a gathering to put all the parts together and appreciate the painting in its original form.

Gus crosses in and out again. Tammy is propelled on stage. She is nervous. At the bell, only Helen, Tammy and Jo remain on stage.

Singer/Yoko: The gathering — which we will call "The Yoko Ono Project" — will begin — *now.*

Sound: Ting of Wishing Bell.

The three women look at each other and the pieces of paper, then look out. Like deer in the traffic headlights. Stop.

A flash, blinding, a tear in the film of reality, when performers are audience and audience part of the performance.

Wait. Wait. Nothing happens.

Singer/Yoko: Congratulations!

Helen: Is this a joke?

Singer/Yoko: You are one of 10,000 selected individuals to whom we have sent this "Part Painting" by Yoko Ono.

Jo: Shhh!

Singer/Yoko: Each person has received a portion of this painting. On *(Date of performance.)* we are holding a gathering to put all the parts together and appreciate the painting in its original form.

Helen: Right. Sure. Where are the other nine-thousand, nine hundred and ninety-seven?

Singer/Yoko: The gathering — which we will call "The Yoko Ono Project" — will begin — *now.*

Sound: Ting of bell.

Tammy and Jo look out and 'see' the audience. Terror. The awful awkward panic of the non-performer on stage.

Helen: Oh, this is great, just great. I'm not a kid any more, Gus. I work, I go home, I eat, sleep, and in the few hours between dinner and bedtime, I'm supposed to cram in everything else that I really want to be doing with my life, and you have to drag me here to this sorry Yoko Ono thing, and if this isn't enough — Gus? Gus?!

Helen looks, 'sees' audience.

Helen: Oh. Uhm. I, uh.... Excuse me ...

Tammy: *(To audience, holding a "Part Painting".)* Uhm, I, I, I was wondering.... Do you have one of these?

Jo: I read about this. The "Part Painting". I just never imagined it quite *this* way.

Jo fumbles for a cigarette. Tammy smiles nervously out to the audience ...

Tammy: Hey, uhh, could I bum one off you?

Helen: *(Cough of protest.)*

Tammy: We are allowed to smoke here, right? I mean, there's an ashtray here and everything ...

Helen walks away disgusted. Jo and Tammy light up, and smoke nervously.

Jo: You don't look like a smoker.

Tammy: Everybody says that. Why do they say that? I mean, what does a smoker look like, you know? *(Pause.)* When I was young, I looked even younger and I'd get hit on by all these guys who were like too afraid to hit on the real women, you know.

Jo: Yeah.

Tammy: They were nice guys and everything but they weren't, you know, what I was looking for.... I'd just light up a cigarette — poof! they were gone.

Tammy and Jo take deep deep drags.

Helen: Do you need me? Can I go now?

Jo: No, I don't think so.

Tammy: What about you?

Jo: Why do I smoke?

Tammy: Yeah, sure, like, I guess.

Jo: I smoke because it's *bad*. And I like it.

Slide: Smoke Piece [14]

Smoke everything you can.
Including your pubic hair.
(y.o., 1964)

Helen: *(To audience.)* Would all the smokers in the room please stand. Would those of you who smoke because it's bad, please raise your hands? Would those of you who smoke because you *like* it, raise your hands. Thank you. Would all the nonsmokers who find this discussion irrelevant, please smack the smoker nearest to you. Thank you.

Jo: Are you finished?

Helen: When I was a kid, my mother used to smoke in
                the bathroom. We all knew. My brother was a
                baby, three years old, and he didn't speak at all.
                My parents were worried maybe something was
                wrong. He would just sit there, all day, staring
                and sucking his thumb. Then one day, Daddy
                comes home and my brother looks up, takes his
                hands out of his mouth and says a full sentence.
                A full sentence: "Mommy smokes in the
                bathroom." Just like that. My mother tells that
                story over and over as proof of my brother's
                genius.... There. Can we go now?

Jo butts out her cigarette. Grinds it in the floor.

Helen: What? It's a true story. I just don't think
                smoking is the smartest form of protest, okay? I
                don't see why you make it into some noble act
                of feminist empowerment. It's just stupid. It
                gives you cancer, wrecks your skin, stains your
                teeth. It's gross, okay? It's just gross.

*Helen turns her back on Jo and Tammy, but can't stand the
gaze of the audience. She turns her back to the audience.*

Tammy: I keep trying to quit but it's really hard, eh? My
                doctor says it's bad but it's even worse if you're
                on the pill so, uhm, like ...

*Helen opens door of the "Danger Box". She considers it for
a moment, then, yes, she steps in. She hides, and sighs with
relief as she closes the lid.*

Sound: (Tape loop.) Yoko's box ... Yoko's box ...

*Jo and Tammy look over to "Danger Box", which has
suddenly started glowing, rumbling, burping ...*

Tammy: Yeah. So.

Scene 13:   BAGism #1

Music: Early Yoko style: Improvisational mood piece.

"Danger Box" glows with Helen Yoko inside, transformed. Three bags in neat piles upstage.

Helen Yoko: I was ... I didn't ... when people visited ... I wanted to be in a big box, a box with little holes so nobody could see me. So you can be inside and see outside but they can't see you.[15]

Jo Yoko walks very slowly to her bag, moving in a slow and extended manner, arranges fabric.

Slide: "BAGISM"

Jo Yoko enters bag. Rolls, shifts, her body shape and attitude masked by the fabric.

Jo Yoko: Bagism: Hiding as performance. As protest. Imagine. Imagine. What is happening here. Inside. I am here. Where are you?

Jo rolls. Stops. Rolls. Freezes. Percussive stop.

Scene 14:   BAGism #2

Tammy: Wow.

David, excited, drags Tammy to bags.

David: Come on. We have to do this. We have to.

Tammy: No, please ... David ...

David: Take off your shoes.

Tammy: What if someone sees us?

David: This is a Yoko Ono thing. Come on.

They place their shoes to the side then climb into a large bag. Giggling comes from the bag. There's movement within the bag.

Tammy: David! Not here! David!

David: Shhhhh.

More movement, more giggling.

Jo Yoko: *(Pops head out of bag)* It's not a game, you know. It's art.

Tammy: Oh.

Jo Yoko drops back into bag. Gus walks over, sees an empty bag beside Jo's. He crawls inside, looking over at Jo's bag. He settles himself then wiggles his way across stage towards Jo.

Scene 15:   Bed in for Peace

Video: Footage of John and Yoko at "Bed-in for Peace".[16]

Slide: WAR IS OVER!

If you want it.
Happy Christmas from John and Yoko.[17]

Music: "Give Peace a Chance".[18]

Tammy's head pops out of bag.

Tammy: I like the bed-ins, "The Peace Campaign". I like that a lot. It was a great idea. Having a bed-in for peace. In the photos, they look so calm, so innocent and enthusiastic. You couldn't do that in this new millennium. A press conference for peace. In a bed. People would laugh. Mind you they probably did then too.

"Bed-in for Peace", Yoko Ono, 1969
Hilton Hotel, Amsterdam
Lenono Photo Archive © 2002 Yoko Ono
Photo by: Ruud Hoff

They look good together. They already kind of look like each other. It's the hair, and the way they hold their mouths. It's something in their eyes. Isn't it weird how couples start to look like each other after a while? John and Yoko. They really loved each other ...

I don't know why people gave them such a hard time. It's hard enough to find love, much less in matching colors. Why can't people understand that?

David's head pops up. He is smiling.

David: Hey, Tammy ...

Tammy and David slide back into the bag.

Production Photo — Bruce Beaton and Keira Loughran.

Photo by Heather Morton

Scene 16:   Yellow Talk[19]

Slide: A, B, or C / Yellow Talk

Lights up on Helen in "Danger Box".

Helen Yoko: Please choose the correct answer. A, B, C, or D. Thank you.

A) All colors are imaginary except yellow. Other colors are shades of yellow in varying degrees which have been given names, as if each existed independently — purely for ideological reasons.
B) Yellow is the only imaginary color.
C) All colors have yellow in it.

D) All colors are imaginary.

I will repeat the choices once.

Helen Yoko speaks briskly.

A) All colors are imaginary except yellow.
B) Yellow is the only imaginary color.
C) All colors have yellow in it.
D) All colors are imaginary.

She looks at her watch, then at the audience, then her watch. Waits ...

Helen Yoko: Thank you. Your time is up.

A stunned silence. Then ...

David and Tammy: Ahhh ... 'D'! The answer is 'd'!

David and Tammy laugh, very silly. Gus smiles at Jo from his bag. Jo rebuffs him. Everyone is now in a bag or a box. Silence, stillness. One by one they emerge from their bags into Avant Garde Heaven ...

Scene 17:   Meeting at Indica

Slide: Indica Gallery, London 1966

Film: Bottoms, Film No. 4[20]

Singer/Yoko: Welcome to 1966. "The Beatles," says John Lennon, "are more popular than Jesus Christ." Beatles LP *Revolver* hits the top of the charts. Bible belt Christians burn Beatles albums. Beatles flee Manila, return to London. London ... Welcome to London. Welcome to the Indica Gallery, London, November 9, 1966. The day before Yoko Ono's first major London exhibit: *Yoko Ono. Yoko Ono.*

Slide: Photo of Yoko at Indica, 1966.[21]

Helen/Yoko and Jo/Yoko bring a ladder on stage. They place it upright on the foor and arrange the bags. They are working hard and are nervous about the exhibit.

Jo Yoko: Dust, canvas and paint cans everywhere.... White walls. White canvases. Yoko Ono ...

Tammy Yoko: Me?

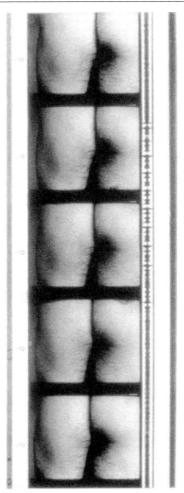

Film No. 4 (Bottoms)
Yoko Ono, 1965, 16mm black and white, sound, 80 minutes
Lenono Photo Archive © 2002 Yoko Ono

Jo Yoko:	... a few artist friends, putting the final touches on the exhibit. A man arrives.
David/John:	Man, lanky white guy, in a groovy sixties outfit, saunters in. Man wanders. Looking closely at things.

David/John examines "Apple".[22]

Helen Yoko:	Yoko acknowledges him but goes on with her tasks.

David/John takes a bite of "Apple".

All Yokos:	Hey!
Jo Yoko:	He's enjoying himself. The privacy ...
Video: the	*P.O.V. of "Ceiling Painting", approaching ladder, going up ... etc.*
David/John:	Man sees a ladder and canvas on ceiling. A magnifying glass hanging down. Man climbs ladder.
Slide:	*"Ceiling Painting"*[23]
Tammy Yoko:	He's kind of cute, really.
Helen Yoko:	He looks, reads. It says, 'yes'.
Jo Yoko:	Yes ...
Helen Yoko:	Yes ...
Tammy Yoko:	Yes ...
David/John:	This is daft!
Jo Yoko:	He's engaged by the work. Excited. He is drawn to another work.
Slide:	*Image of "Painting To Hammer A Nail In"*[24]
Tammy Yoko:	It's called: "Painting to Hammer a Nail In".
Helen Yoko:	He looks for nails. Can't find any.
David/John:	You're the artist?
3 Yokos:	Yes.
David:	Well, listen, I want to hammer in a nail. It says right here: 'hammer in a nail.'

"Ceiling Painting (YES Painting)", Yoko Ono, 1966
Text on paper, glass metal frame, metal chain, painting ladder
Collection of the artist © 2002 Yoko Ono
Photo by: Oded Lobi

Tammy Yoko:	I can't allow that, no.
Jo Yoko:	The exhibit hasn't opened yet so I —
David/John:	But I want to hammer in a nail.
3 Yokos:	No.
David/John:	I want to hammer in a nail.
3 Yokos:	No.
David/John:	I really want to hammer in a nail.
3 Yokos:	I said, N0.
Jo Yoko:	The gallery owner pulls Yoko aside —
Gus/Man:	Look, this guy's a big rock star, he's you know, you know ...
Tammy Yoko:	Who?
Gus/Man:	A millionaire, he's a millionaire. Yoko, let him hammer in a nail. Maybe he'll buy the painting. Let the rich bugger hammer in a fucking nail, Yoko!
Tammy Yoko:	Oh, alright. If you give me five shillings, you can hammer in a nail.
David/John:	Well, if I give you an imaginary five shillings, can I hammer in an imaginary nail?
Jo Yoko:	Man and Yoko exchange a smile, a look —
Tammy Yoko:	Powerful.
Jo Yoko:	Contact has been made.
Helen Yoko:	And that's how it all started.

Video: Psychedelics shifting to ...[25]

Scene 18:   Two Virgins

Image: John and Yoko, Two Virgins *cover art,*[26] *censored.*

Helen Yoko: Gloria Steinem. *Cosmopolitan Magazine,*
                December 1964. "Feature Schwartz, ex-
                secretary of the Beatles Fan Club of America,
                discovered that the average Beatles fan is white,
                13-17 years old, of middle-class background,
                weighs 105-140 pounds, owns a transistor radio
                with an earplug attachment and has Beatles
                photographs plastered all over her room."

Jo Yoko: Yoko Ono, 31, 96 pounds, upper-class
                background, Japanese neo-Buddhist Fluxus
                artist, no appliances, one child.

Scene 19:   A Good Match

Music: "Good Match" — Pui Ming's Version

Film: Film loop of a match being lit and burning out.

Singer/Yoko: *(Looping underneath.)*

                Yoko Ono: Born February 18, 1933.
                Aquarius. Water Rooster.
                John Lennon: Born October 9, 1940.
                Libra. Metal Dragon.
                A good match ... A good match ... A good
                match ...

Jo Yoko: Around the time that I met John, I went to a
                palmist, and he said, he said you are like a very
                very fast wind that goes speeding around the
                world. The only thing you don't have is a root.
                But you have met a person who is fixed like a

mountain, and if you get connected to this
mountain, you might just materialize.[27]

Lights fading up on David and Tammy necking in a corner.

Tammy: David, you're such a guy ...

Tammy and David continue necking.

Scene 20:   Kiss Kiss Kiss

Music: "Kiss Kiss Kiss"

Movement beginning as a gentle duet between Tammy and David. Jo enters, pursued by Gus, tentative, flirtatious, increasingly percussive. Helen enters. An accidental and aggressive confrontation occurs between Helen and Jo. The women are left on stage, orgasmic yet still, fading to darkness as Yoko comes, and comes, and comes ...

Scene 21:   Part Painting 3

Slide: "Part Painting"

A growing heap of "Part Paintings". The three women are on stage in fixed positions. Gus and David enter and exit.

Singer/Yoko: Congratulations! You are one of 10,000 selected individuals to whom we have sent this "Part Painting" by Yoko Ono.

Helen: *(Sarcastic.)* Wow.

Singer/Yoko: Each person has received a portion of this painting. On *(Date of performance.)* we are

	holding a gathering to put all the parts together and appreciate the painting in its original form.
Jo:	*(To Tammy.)* Smoke?
Tammy:	Thanks.
Singer/Yoko:	The gathering — which we will call "The Yoko Ono Project" — will begin — *now.*

Sound: Ting of Wishing Bell.

Pause. The women see the audience. They watch the audience, acknowledge the audience and, though they gradually relax, they remain wary.

Tammy:	Jo.
Jo:	Yeah.
Tammy:	You're Korean, right?
Jo:	Yup.
Tammy:	Have you ever gone out with a Korean guy? You know, gone out like gone out?
Jo:	No.
Helen:	I, is there someone here who can stop this? I'm very, I'm ... *(To audience.)* I'd really like to go now.

Helen, receiving no response, turns her back to the audience and sits in frustration.

Tammy:	I was just wondering, eh. I have a couple of Chinese and Korean girlfriends, they're not girlfriends really, they're girls I know, women, I mean. Mostly our parents know each other, that kind of thing. Anyway, none of them are going out with Chinese guys either. It's weird, eh? You'd think that, uhm ... *(To Helen.)* Hey, uhm ...
Helen:	Helen. My name's Helen.
Tammy:	Helen. Helen, have you? Have you ever, you know, gone out with an Asian guy?

Helen:	Have you?
Tammy:	No, I was just saying, I was just telling Jo. I just started this relationship thing, and I got to thinking how most of my friends, the women I know who are Chinese and stuff don't really go with Chinese guys ... So I was, like, wondering, if you have ever, you know, gone out with a guy who's, you know, Japanese or Korean or you know, Chinese ... like.

Helen stares, refusing to answer.

	'Cause, like, there's a lot of pressure, eh? A lot of pressure to go out with Chinese guys. My Mom, like, she keeps setting me up with sons of her friends, they're nice guys and all, but they're not, like, what I'm looking for.
Jo:	Rhodes scholars, lawyers, accountants, doctors in training.
Tammy:	Yeah!
Jo:	I know.
Tammy:	You do?
Jo:	Yeah. My mother did the same thing. They just never worked out.
Tammy:	God, I thought I was the only one.
Jo:	No.
Helen:	There's nothing wrong with Asian guys.
Tammy:	No, no, I didn't mean that. It's just, you know, the pressure. You know, the pressure to, you know —
	I mean, I've had crushes on Asian guys. This one guy, he was from Trinidad. This Trini-Chinese sculptor with the warmest voice. God, he'd say hello and I'd just, like, melt. It turned out he was gay. But we're friends and

	everything, but, you know, it's kind of, you know ...
Jo:	All the cool Asian men are gay.
Tammy:	Well, no, that's not true. I've met a few cool guys who are straight. But they're, like, taken or, you know —
Jo:	Too young.
Tammy:	Yeah.

Helen looks at her watch. Taps it.

Tammy:	Do you think Jason Scott Lee is gay?
Jo:	Oh, probably.
Singer/Yoko:	The gathering which we will call the "Yoko Ono Project", will begin *NOW* — will begin *NOW* — will begin*NOW*.
Helen:	I find this all very stressful.
Jo:	What? Talking about men?
Helen:	I, I, no. That's not what I meant.
Tammy:	Hey, Helen? Helen, you never said. Have you, like, ever gone out with an Asian guy?
Helen:	Well, I, you see — the only Asian guy in my high school was my brother. Not that I ... I mean ... there wasn't much selection, and I'm too busy to think about ... that now ... so.
Jo:	No. The answer is no.
Tammy:	What about them? Do you think they — *(To audience)* Hi. Uhm. Would all the Asian women in the audience please stand. *(Jo whispers in her ear.)* Oh, okay. Would all the Asian women stand, and could everybody else please cover their eyes. Hey! You too! No cheating.
Jo:	You'll hear the results when it's over.
Tammy:	Thank you. Now, would those of you who have

had a relationship with an Asian guy ... *(Jo whispers.)* with an Asian *partner*, please raise your hands. Are you first or second generation? Okay. And if the relationship was good, or significant, like, you know, longer than a month, could you raise your hands again.

Jo: Hey! Eyes covered.

Tammy: Thank you.

Alternate text: use as necessary:

Tammy: Please, this is a Yoko thing.

Jo: You're just lucky *you're* not up here.

Alternate text: if two women side-by-side raise their hands.

Jo: Can I ask, are you two together. I see.

Tammy: What? *(Jo whispers.)* Really? Oh.

Resume with:

Tammy: And how many of you are in those relationships now? *(Jo whispers.)* And Jo would like to know how many of you have had crushes on Asian men who turned out to be gay? Thank you. *(Jo whispers.)* And we'd like to apologize for the — *(Jo whispers.)* for the heterosexual bias of this survey. Sorry. Uhm. Thank you. You can sit now. Everyone ... at ease.

Jo: *(Number)* Asian women, most of whom were probably second-generation. *(Number.)* have had a good or significant relationship with another Asian. Of those *(Number.)* were good relationships, and *(Number.)* are still in those relationships. *(Number.)* women have had crushes on gay Asian men. Counting me.

Alternate text, use as necessary:

Jo: And get this: according to US Census reports, we'll just have to assume the figures in Canada are similar, according to US Census reports, from 1960 to 1990, white-Asian couples increased tenfold, and of those interracial marriages, 72 per cent were white male-Asian female couples. A survey of local famous Asian women — Adrienne Clarkson, Evelyn Lau, Jan Wong, Jane Luk —

Tammy: She's "Smokey"!

Jo: Brenda Kamino —

Tammy: Is she famous?

Jo: She *ought* to be. Anyway, they're all going out with, or have mostly gone out with, are married to, or whatever, to white guys. All of them.

Resume with:

Tammy: Wow. So, like, Asian women, second-generation Asian women, like hardly ever go out with Asian men. I mean, I thought, I didn't really believe it was a *trend.*

Jo: Believe it, girl.

Helen: My brother went out with an Asian girl.

Jo: Is he cool?

Helen: He's my brother.

Jo: So she dumped him.

Helen: No, they broke up.

Jo: Right. Where was she from?

Helen: Calgary.

Jo: Second-generation?

Helen:	She's from Calgary. It happens sometimes. Maybe not often. But sometimes. Once and a while.
Jo:	Hmmmph. Well, I've never seen it.
Helen:	*(Mutters inaudibly.)* Close-minded pretentious little bitch.
Jo:	Excuse me?
Helen:	Nothing, nothing. I didn't say anything ... I take it back.
Tammy:	Can we get back to this? Okay, so, like, Asian women, second-generation Asian women, do not go out with Asian men because: One. Poor selection. It's hard to meet, and stuff. Two. A lot of the cool Asian guys are gay. Three —
Jo:	Asian guys don't go for rebellious Asian women. *(Pause.)* It goes without saying.
Tammy:	Okay. Uhm, where was I? Four —
Jo:	Fucking an Asian guy is like fucking your brother.
Helen:	Wait a second.
Tammy:	We didn't talk about that, did we?
Helen:	That is way out of line! Are you saying —? You're saying —? Look, I never said that! I never said that! You're just trying to make me look stupid. You've been doing it the whole time. Well, fuck you.
Tammy:	Helen! Helen, please.
Jo:	Get a grip, girl. We're just discussing men. You have a problem with that?
Helen:	Oh, you're so cool, aren't you? So worldly and above us all. Well, fuck you and your coolness.
Jo:	Yeah, well, fuck you and your uptight Mother Superior act, okay? I don't know what your problem is but every time anyone mentions the word *men*, or *art*, or *Yoko Ono* you — *(Helen*

edges very close, threatening. Jo does not back down.) Don't start, Helen. Don't you start! Don't you fucking start with me lady!

Helen: *(Charging head first at Jo.)* BiiiiTTTCCCHHHH!

Jo: FUCK YOU!

Helen and Jo fight — punching, screaming, kicking, biting, hair pulling and so on.

Tammy: Stop! Oh, please stop! No, NO! Please, please, please, stop! Please! Oh, please, please stop! Both of you. I'm begging. *(Final sustained wail of desperation.)* PLEEEAAAASSSSEEE!!!!!!

Tammy's scream reaches an ear-splitting peak. All lights snap out. Utter and sudden silence. Nothing happens.

Singer/Yoko: *(Faint.)* Congratulations. You are one of ten thousand selected individuals — ten thousand selected individuals — ten thousand selected individuals ...

In darkness, silence and then moans.

Helen: What happened?

Jo: You went ballistic.

Helen: I mean after that.

Jo: I don't know. Someone turned off the lights.

Breathing is heard, then a rustle of clothing, followed by a cough. Nothing happens.

Tammy: Helen?

Helen: Yeah, I'm here.

Tammy: Jo?

Jo: Uh hunh.

Tammy: I was thinking, you know, it's kinda weird, this this this thing, hanging with other Asian women. It's sort of like seeing someone wearing your clothes. Or hearing someone tell you they dreamt the same dream you had the night before. You know what I mean? I've kind of gotten used to being the only one. Jo? Jo? Helen?

Silence. Silence. Silence.

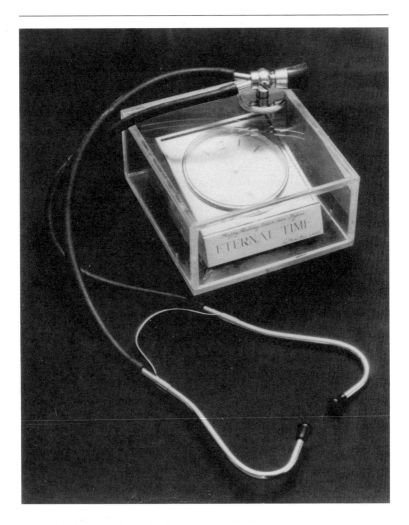

"Eternal Time, 1966", Yoko Ono
Unfinished Paintings and Objects, Indica Gallery, London, 1966
Photo by: Iain Macmillan
Courtesy of Lenono Photo Archive
Black and white, 8" x 10" still

Scene 22:   Eternal Time aka Technical Difficulties

All slightly askew, Hal in 2001: A Space Odyssey *as he's being switched off, wonky, as if every element including Singer/Yoko were doped ...*

Slide: Photo of Yoko Ono's "Eternal Time" — a sculpture featuring a clock with no hour or minute hands with a stethoscope attached.

Slide: "Eternal Time Clock", 1965[28]

Singer/Yoko: Time, eternal time, one big piece of sky passing without sound, the time is passing, the time is past, the time is now ...

Sound: Ting! Tick. Tick. Tick. Tick ...

Singer/Yoko: Time, eternal time, one big piece of sky, passing without sound, the time is passing, the time is past, the time is now ...

Sound: Ting! Tick. Tick. Tick. Tick....

Singer/Yoko: Time, eternal time.... All my work is a form of wishing ...*[29]* I thought art, I thought art was a verb, rather than a noun, a noun ...[30]

Music: "Part Painting Theme," wonky, technical difficulties, scratch of radio dial spinning ...

Singer/Yoko: To appreciate the painting ... to appreciate ... to appreciate, in its original form ... begin *now.*

Gus struggles to get on stage. He struggles against obstructions.

Singer/Yoko: *(As if on speed.)* All colors are imaginary except yellow.
Yellow is the only imaginary color.
All colors have yellow in it.
All colors are imaginary.

Gus finally lands, centre stage.

Sound: Ting!

All lights, images and video fade to black.[31]

Scene 23:   Gus's Excellent Rant

The stage is completly black. Gus is centre stage. The three women are dishevelled and scattered about the stage.

Gus: *(To the booth.)* Excuse me! Can I have some light here! Hello!! I have something to say, do you mind? Five minutes, just give me five fucking minutes, okay! *(Spotlight on Gus.)* Thank you.

Can someone tell me why Asian women who *find* feminism assume that their liberation is a license to shit on their yellow brothers? Hunh? Can someone please explain this to me? *Joy Luck Club, Double Happiness* — not one decent, straight Asian guy. We get shit on by Hollywood. Corporate America broadcasts images of us as geeks, Holy Chow, Mista Brow, preez come dis way. Or evil opium smoking ganglords, Kung-Fu terrorists that end up dead by the end of one scene. Or, yeah, *Sixteen Candles*, freaky skirt-chasing creepizoids — and Asian women swallow it whole and spit back this shit that yellow guys aren't good enough. They want some swanky white dude, a guy with a jeep and a skintight Speedo swimsuit, some McDude who plays guitar and sings country and western songs.

(To Jo.) Well, listen up, sister, maybe you're not so independently-minded as you think. Maybe you're just another gullible media victim whose been swayed by the evil powers of Hollywood. Maybe you've got secret pockets of internalized racism, and you don't want to be seen with a yellow dude.

We're your brothers, your cousins, your classmates — and we're not good enough for you? Me, I'm not good enough for you?

Tammy:	Would you like some water?
Gus:	No! Thank you. You know, I came here thinking, Yoko Ono, she's cool, she was a ground-breaker, kind of curious you know, and yeah, maybe I was thinking, I might meet some people, get to talking, see where that might lead, but you know what? Chicks like you are unfuckably unbelievable, and I wouldn't fuck you if you — well no, I would, but I wouldn't if I had a choice.
Jo:	Who are you?
Gus:	Gus. Gus. My name's Gus.
Helen:	He's my brother.
Jo:	Gus, do you know where you are?
Gus:	You know what? I don't like you.
Jo:	You know what? I don't care if you don't like me.

Pause.

Gus:	Really?
Jo:	Really.
Gus:	You know what? I don't think that's true. I think you're so afraid people won't like you, in this case me, that you spend a lot of time on, what shall I call it, your presentation, your costume, your mannerisms, even the kind of art you like to dislike. Because inside you're scared shitless. I'll bet you've dumped every guy you've dated just so he wouldn't have the chance to dump you first.
Jo:	Lemon. Yellow on the outside, yellow on the inside, and bitter, bitter, bitter.
Gus:	Yeah? Well tell me something about yourself. Come on. Tell me something *real*. Something I could only know about you if you told me. Not

about Yoko, or her art, no offence, but about you. Come on. Come on, Jo!

Jo storms off.

Scene 24:   Cut Piece

Slides: "Cut Piece"; Images of Yoko performing "Cut Piece", increasingly exposed.

Jo enters with scissors.

Jo: "Cut Piece". It was first performed by Yoko Ono in Kyoto, 1964. She comes on the stage, and in a sitting position, places a pair of scissors in front of her. She asks the audience to come up on the stage, one by one, and cut a portion of her clothing (anywhere they like) and take it.[32] *(Jo sits. Jo waits. And waits.)* The piece ends when all the clothing is cut.

Jo waits, for an uncomfortably long time. One by one, Helen, David and Tammy approach and cut parts of her blouse. Gus stands nervously.

Singer/Yoko: And people went on cutting the parts they did not like of me, finally there was only the stone remained of me that was in me but they still were not satisfied and wanted to know what it's like in the stone ...[33]

Jo: Is this, is this, is this it? I feel, I want, I, I, I — I just want, I just I want, I just, I just want, I just want ... I just want to be, to be, to be ...

David: Is this a Yoko thing?

Gus: Shhhhh!!!!

"Cut Piece", Yoko Ono, 1965
Performance at Carnegie Recital Hall, New York
Lenono Photo Archive © 2002 Yoko Ono
Photo by: Minoru Niizuma

Gus walks over, and protectively drapes his jacket over Jo's shoulders. Jo throws it off — then draws it in, clutches it, weeping. Gus gently removes the scissors. He sits, watching Jo.

Scene 25:   Whisper Piece[34]

Slide: "Whisper Piece"

Gus: He wants a dialogue, wants to know if Jo would be interested in going out with him, give him an opportunity to disprove her low opinion of yellow dudes because well, she's kind of cute.

Helen: Must basically send on the message with one word deleted and one conjunction changed. As she wishes.

David: Must add one sweet nothing to Tammy.

Tammy: Must try and make it seem nicer than it is, and maybe smooth it over. Cheats. Says something to David. She needs to talk. Something about her mom ...

Jo: Jo must announce what she hears.

Gus: No, I said, *"(Whatever he first whispered to Helen)."* So? Are we on?

Jo: I, I ... I'll think about it.

Scene 26:   Walking On Thin Ice

Music: "Walking on Thin Ice"[35]

The actors burst into edgy movement — walking, travelling in isolation, enacting images of urban alienation and danger. All characters continue striding and circling, until only David and Tammy are left on stage.

Tammy is distraught, David confused.

David: *(To Tammy.)* What is it? *(To audience.)* Excuse us.

Tammy: David, it's just, I know I should have told you, I've just been kind of tense you know, I just needed to clear my head.

David: But your mom?

Tammy: Yeah, my mom's kind of unstable right now. I mean, she *knows.* And like, I haven't been home for a few days. You know, since I saw you...? We had a major parental blowout, eh.

David: She really doesn't like me, does she?

Tammy: Yeah. I mean, she hates you, I mean she hates the idea of you. You know? I mean, she doesn't hate you, how can she hate you, when she's never even met you ... right?

Oh God, it's just crazy right now. I mean, I can hardly sleep 'cause I'm staying at Caroline's on the sofa, and my mother is calling at all hours and the phone's in Caroline's bedroom, right? It's awful. And Caroline doesn't want to turn off the phone because Michael's sick, right, and there might be an emergency. She's really nice about it, but you know, like, I don't want to overstay my welcome, you know? It's just that I don't really have a place to stay. I mean, I sneak home in the day, get clean clothes and then

	sneak out again. It's just, I mean, I have essays due next week and school and —
David:	Stay at my place. I want you to. Stay at my place. Tammy, you're so small, you hardly take up any room at all.

Scene 27:   Line Talk

Slide: "Line Talk"

Jo Yoko:	Line Talk:
	A line is — a sick circle. a billion lines cluttered into a very narrow space. An unfolded word. An aggressive dot.[36]
	Draw a line with yourself. Go on drawing until you disappear.[37]
	What is a circle event?

Scene 28:   Not Microscopic

David:	What *is* a circle event?
Tammy:	David, David, I don't know, David, listen to me. This is important, like, David. David, if I come to your place, I'll take up room. I'm not a hard

person to live with, but, like, I *will* take up room. And sometimes, I might take up *a lot* of room, you know?

I mean, my make-up will be shoved next to your shaving cream, and sometimes, maybe I'll take over the kitchen table to write my essays, and maybe maybe maybe I'll be on the phone when you are expecting a call and it'll make you crazy. Or I'll want to be alone, you know? I'll take up lots of room. I'm small but I'm not *microscopic*!

David: Okay.

Tammy: Okay?

David: Yeah. Okay. I was actually thinking I could build a loft, you know, in that front room, clear some space for a study for you. I already bought some paint 'cause I know you think the kitchen walls are kind of crummy, and if I get rid of the bike rack —

Tammy: David. You know what?

David: What?

Tammy kisses him.

Tammy: I love you.

David: I love you too.

Scene 29:   Part Painting 4

Lights up. The three women are each standing in a massive, knee-high pile of "Part Paintings".

Singer/Yoko: Congratulations! You are one of 10,000 selected individuals to whom we have sent —

Production Photo — Keira Loughran, M.J. Kang, Denise Fujiwara.

Photo: Heather Morton

Helen:	OH NO! Not again! not again, not again, oh no, oh no, onoonoono *(Continues under.)*
Singer/Yoko:	— this "Part Painting" by Yoko Ono. Each person has received a portion of this painting —
Jo:	*(To Tammy.)* Deja vu, eh?
Singer/Yoko:	— On *(Date of performance.)* we are holding a gathering to put all the parts together and appreciate the painting in its original form.
Jo:	*(Holding out handful of "Part Paintings".)* Oh!
Singer/Yoko:	The gathering, which we will call "The Yoko Ono Project", will begin NOW.
Helen:	*(An obsessive moan.)* ono -ono-onoono, oh no not again! Oh no, ono ono oh NO! *(Helen's scream suddenly builds, peaks into a scream weirdly reminiscent of Yoko's emotional vocal blowouts.)* OOOOOONNO, OONNOO!!

Silence. Collapse.

Jo:	*(Dropping the "Part Paintings".)* These are beginning to add up.
Helen:	*(Small whimper.)*
Tammy:	*(Gestures to Helen.)* Hey, do you think she's okay?
Jo:	She just needs to chill a bit.... Damn, I'm out of smokes!
Singer/Yoko:	Congratulations!

Helen rises, desperately agitated. Jo and Tammy stare out into the audience, less tense and threatened than before, but still on their guard.

Helen:	Oh, no ... not again, not again ...
Singer/Yoko:	You are one of 10,000 selected individuals to whom we have sent this "Part Painting" by Yoko Ono.

Helen:	*(Curls into herself. Moans obsessively.)* "Oh-no ono ono onononon ..." *(Continues under.)*
Singer/Yoko:	Each person has received a portion of this painting. On *(Date of performance.)* we are holding a gathering to put all the parts together and appreciate the painting in its original form. The gathering — which we will call "The Yoko Ono Project" — will begin n*ow*.
Helen:	*(Her scream builds, builds, then peaks. Primitive primeval despair. She collapses.)*

Blackout.

Production Photo (Vancouver Firehall) — Donna Yamamoto.

Photo by Janet Baxter

Scene 30:   BAGism #3

Music: "Mind Holes"[38]

*Lights up on three women in front of bags. They are drawn
to the bags. They touch them, pick them up, and move the
bags. Heavy, the bags are so heavy. They each look in their
bag then stop. Jo looks up, smiling. She looks down, still
smiling. Tammy looks, curiously. Helen, in a bag, looks up,
a gives a silent scream.*

*Fade on Helen screaming, getting sucked into the bag,
rolling in bag, into the "Danger Box".*

Scene 31:   Danger Box

*The lid of the "Danger Box" rises, and Helen emerges, dusty
and coughing, traumatized.*

Helen: Dusty air, pinchy place, my memory maybe, all
                    these bits and pieces coming together like iron
                    filings around a magnet — *Rolling Stone,
                    Village Voice, People Magazine, Esquire* —
                    things I must have read, how they despised her
                    — the root of why I feel so — God, this is hard
                    for me — I'm beginning to understand her art
                    and how that's all connected ... why they hate
                    her, they hate her.

*Slide: Cartoon of huge Yoko with little bug John Lennon on
a leash.*[39]

Helen: *Esquire Magazine*, December 1970. "John
                    Rennon's Excrusive Gloupie. On the load to
                    briss with the Yoko nobody Onos." Charming.

Slide: Cover of People Magazine, *December 1988.*

Helen:	"Under Yoko's Spell. Scenes of despair, drugs and domination by his wife."

And the adjectives:

Ugly, obnoxious, domineering, pretentious, abrasive, aggressive, infantalizing, untalented, obsessive, cold, cruel, unpleasant, unattractive.... It goes on and on ...

Lennon says: "After I started seeing Yoko, I would get these hateful letters, cruel things. 'That Japanese witch will slit your throat in the night'. I love her. Nobody seems to believe me."

He loved her. They loved each other. She is Asian. She isn't a subservient geisha girl. She isn't a groupie. She isn't a Brigitte Bardot wannabe. She is just herself. That's what it's all about. That she is just herself ... and so they hate her. And so they hate me. And so I hated her too.

Helen sinks back into the "Danger Box". It glows, shakes and fades.

Scene 32:   Rising

Image: Cover of Rising

Music: "Rising"[40]

Helen Yoko:	*Watch Magazine*, Toronto, January 1996.

"This album reinforces the argument that Mark David Chapman (the guy who shot Lennon) could have saved us all a lot of grief by just aiming one foot to the right." [41]

Sound: Opening of "No": Four gunshots. Scream 'No!'[42]

Scene 33: Tammy and David

Tammy: Somebody wrote that? Here, in Toronto?!!

David: Tammy, it's okay. You don't need to get upset. I mean —

Tammy: No, no, I do need to get upset. I do. People shouldn't be so stupid, and mean, and arrogant, and cruel. Because we're talking about love, right, cause you know, I *love* you. I need to be upset, David, okay, because my mom is saying how she wishes I'd never been born, because I'm in love with you, do you understand? And I love my Mom, and the idea of anything happening to you or to my mom, to anyone I love, to someone you love, that they can just leave my life forever like that, oh God, David, she was right there.... Can you imagine? Can you imagine?

Scene 34: Question Piece[43]

Slide: *"Question Piece"*

Singer/Yoko: A dialogue or a monologue of continuous questions, answered only by questions, in any language or in many different languages.

All Actors: *(To audience, divide lines as necessary.)*

                So you're an artist, are you?
                What kind of art do you do?
                Do you call this art?
                What do you mean by this?
                Do you do drugs?
                What kind of drugs do you do?

Marijuana, speed, LSD, heroine?
What about mushrooms? Cocaine?
Would you call yourself an addict?
Would you call yourself a feminist?
Would you call yourself a witch?
Are you a witch?
Is it true you are bearing Lennon's illegitimate child?
Is it true you told Cynthia to fuck off?
Do you think this is funny?
Do you think this is a joke?
Could you speak louder?
Could you shut up?
Could you move to the side?
Do you hate Paul?
Why do you hate Paul?

All: WHAT HAVE YOU DONE TO JOHN!?
          WHAT HAVE YOU DONE TO HIM!?

Video: Fade up in images of John and Yoko, waltzing, laughing, making love. Segue to images of Yoko harassed, hounded, and finally alone.[44]

Scene 35:   Hate/Love ...

Helen Yoko: Hate is a very powerful force. Like love. Love is a very powerful force in this world. Love can change people, situations. Hate is harder. When people hate you, really hate you, you can swallow that hate and use it to make yourself strong ... almost invincible ... like the wind or water. You cannot stop the wind. It will always find its way.[45]

Slow fade to black.

Scene 36:   **"Ono's Sales List"**[46]

Slide: "Ono's Sales List"

Singer/Yoko: Ono's Sales List.

"Self Portrait", $1—. With frame $5—
"Crying Machine", drops tears and cries for you
when coin is deposited. $3,000.

Helen Yoko: "Danger Box", $1,100. "Word Machine", "Sky
Machine", "Eternal Time". A beautiful Eternal
Time Clock that keeps Eternal Time ... $800—

Jo Yoko: Film Scripts, Soundtapes, Garden Sets,
Underwear — Underwear: Special defects
underwear for men, designed to accent your
special defects, $10 in cotton, $175 in Vicuna.
Underwear to make you high — for women.

Tammy Yoko: Paintings — Nail Painting ... Flower Painting ...
Shadow Painting and many other great do-it-
yourself paintings. Fifty dollars.

Music: "Part Painting Theme"

Singer/Yoko: "Part Painting", contains 10,000 parts, $100 per
3 square inch unit details available *upon
request.*

Scene 37:   **Part Painting 5**

Slide: "Part Painting"

Music: "Part Painting Theme" fading to silence.

*This is the Music of the Mind version of "Part Painting".
Whatever choreography, conventions or blocking that has
been established for previous Part Painting scenes should
be repeated here, exactly, as before, but in silence. Actors*

must enter as they did before, reacting as they have before. There are more papers, but no words. If the Singer/Yoko has been lit in previous versions, she should be lit here. She mouths her text, and procedes to the ringing of the bell.

Singer Yoko rings the Wishing Bell.

All lights out.

Scene 38:   Original Form

Helen: I remember, when I was a kid. About twelve. A couple of boys younger than me started chasing me around the school yard calling me 'chink'. I ran home in tears. I didn't know what 'chink' meant but I knew it was dirty. Then I found out what it meant. Chinese. Chinese. I'm not Chinese. But even if I were, so what. Why should that be dirty? So the next time it happened, I started fighting back. I pushed them into a corner and started talking. I said:

You're really stupid, calling me chink. I'm not a chink, and I'm not Chinese and even if I were I'd be proud because the Chinese are smart and they invented the printing press, gun powder, silk and all kinds of things way before Europe did, hundreds of years ahead, and the Chinese have an amazing civilization and art and stuff, but you're too stupid to know that, you're so stupid that you think it's an insult, you're so stupid you don't know how stupid you really are.

Rest.

And I'm telling the principal on you.

Jo: I grew up in Don Mills, you know? I hated it, the

• 68 •

suburbs, I hated being the Korean kid, the way my mom drove like a turtle, hunched over the wheel. I felt stupid all the time, not knowing what to do with all those extra forks and spoons. I was always three steps behind. But Yoko, she has her shit together. She's so so cool and so I just, I just wanted to be like her, you know ...

Tammy: I just want to say, uhm, in these dark times, with all the bombing and war and stuff going on, that it's like more important than ever to, like, believe in peace, you know? Like, Yoko is, like, that what she's been saying all this time, right? Like, peace and art and —

David: — Imagination. Don't forget imagination.

Production photo — M.J. Kang, Denise Fujiwara, Keira Loughran, Glenn Marc Silot, Bruce Beaton.

Photo by Heather Morton

Tammy: Imagination. Exactly. And, like, if you're like, if you're gonna, if you're gonna dis Yoko, you're gonna have to deal with me.

David: And me!

Helen: Yoko. Tell me I remind you of Yoko. Go ahead. Yoko Ono. *(Smiles.)* Yoko Ono.

Image: Yoko Ono with sunglasses.

Helen puts sunglasses on. Messes up her hair.

Sound: (Tape loop.) "Yoko's Box ... Yoko's Box ... Yoko's Box ..."

Helen is joined by Jo and Tammy. Jo and Tammy put on sunglasses and mess up their hair. They make peace signs as "Part Paintings" rain down from above.

Jo: So this is it. The Original Form. This is it. Anarchy. A glorious anarchy.

Tammy: A glorious anarchy.

Helen: That's good.

Music: "Yes, I'm your Angel"[47]

Singer/Yoko: Yes, I'm your angel.
I'll give you everything
in my magic power.
So make a wish.
I'll let it come
true for you.
Tra-la-la-la-la ...

Helen picks up a "Part Painting". Kisses it. Throws it in the air.

Helen: I'm making a wish. Come on!

Tammy giggles, picks up a "Part Painting", kisses it, tosses it. Does it again and again.

Tammy: I keep wishing for the same thing.

Jo laughs, makes a wish. The three of them, wishing. David make wishes and showers them on Tammy. Gus wishes.

Gus: *(To Jo.)* So, Jo-Song, are we on? Friday night?

Jo shakes her head. Gus wishes again. Jo shakes her head. Gus wishes again.

Gus: Jo? Last chance.

Jo: Oh, alright.

Gus wishes again. A secret wish.

Jo: What was that for?

Gus: None of your business.

All turn to Singer/Yoko. She makes a wish.

Singer/Yoko: *(To audience.)* *Your* turn.

All: Make a wish ...

Blackout.

Slide: Fade down on Yoko's image to black.

Singer/Yoko: I am here. Where are you?

The end. Finito.

Yoko Ono
Iain MacMillan/Lenono Photo Archives
black & white photo

YOKO ONO's work

Instruction Poems, Sculptures, Films, Images.

ONO's work is an integral part of the play, and I have attempted, throughout the playscript, to cite accurate information on the original source, date of creation, and/or first public performance, as well as the book, video, recording or publication in which it is easily accessible to the public. There are, however, many points of inspiration that simply cannot be annotated. I urge you to experience for yourself, without mediation, Yoko Ono's Instruction Poems, her music, films, sculptures and installations.

Books

YES YOKO ONO, a 390 page catalogue of Ono's works. Published by the Japan Society and Harry N. Abrams, Inc., New York, N.Y., 2000.

Grapefruit, Works and Drawings by Yoko Ono, Introduction by John Lennon. Published by Simon and Schuster, New York, N.Y. 1964, 1970.

Instruction Paintings, by Yoko Ono. Weatherhill, New York/ Tokyo, 1995.

Yoko Ono: Arias and Objects by Barbara Haskell and John Hanhardt. Peregrine Smith Books, Gibb-Smith Publishers, 1991.

The Ballad of John and Yoko, The Editors of Rolling Stone, edited by Jonathan Cott and Christine Doudna. Rolling Stone Press, Dolphin Books Doubleday and Co., Garden City, N.Y. 1982.

Music

A great deal of Yoko Ono's music, including her stunning early work with Plastic Ono Band, and the six disk *ONOBOX* CD set, has recently been rereleased by Rykodisc. For more information please check their website: http://www.rykodisc.com

Videos

The following films are available on video at speciality video stores and are invaluable starting points in research.

Yoko Ono: Then and Now

John Lennon: Imagine

John and Yoko on the Mike Douglas Show, 1971

Online Resources

For up-to-date information on Yoko resources and links to other online Ono resources please visit:

Richard Joly's ONOWEB http://silence.metatronpress.com/onoweb

Instant Karma http://www.instantkarma.com

The Fluxus Homepage http://www.nutscape.com/fluxus/homepage

Approximately Infinite Universe: A Yoko Ono Box http://www.kaapeli.fi.aiu

Loud Mouth Asian Babes http://www.interlog.com/~jyoon

The Yoko Ono Project includes artworks by Ono indicated by slide titles. Ono texts are *Instruction Poems*, from *Grapefruit* (1964) are indicated by title slides: Lighting Piece, Yellow Talk, Truth/False, Cut Piece, Question Piece, Ono's Sales List and so on. In one or two cases, I have made slight edits to texts for staging purposes. Music by Ono is throughout — all pre-show music, as well as, "O' Wind", "No Bed for Beatle John", "Kiss Kiss Kiss", "Open Your Box", "Walking on Thin Ice", "No No No", "I Don't Know Why", "Remember Love", and "Yes, I'm Your Angel".

1. The full text for the "Part Painting", appears in *Yoko Ono: Arias and Objects* by Barbara Haskell & John Hanhardt, 1991. (p.80). The text here is only a portion and is modified to suit the needs of the play. References to "Part Painting" also occur in *Grapefruit*, in "Ono's Sales List", with portions described as 3" x 3". *Grapefruit,* originally published in a limited edition in 1964, was republished by

Simon and Schuster in 1970. This edition, however, does not have page numbers.

2. LIGHTING PIECE, 1955 autumn. *Grapefruit.*

3. FALLING PIECE, 1964 spring. *Grapefruit.*

4. A reference to BREATHE PIECE, in *Grapefruit*: "First performed at Wesleyan University Conn., U.S.A., in 1966. A large card with small lettering saying 'breathe' was passed three times among the audience."

5. Please see "Yoko Ono and Her Sixteen-Track Voice", by Jonathan Cott, *Rolling Stone*, March 18, 1971; *The Ballad of John and Yoko*, (p. 116).

6. *Liverpool Daily Post*, March 10, 1967.

7, *Rising*, Yoko Ono/IMA, Capitol Records, 1995.

8. "A Hard Day's Night", words and music by John Lennon and Paul McCartney, 1964.

9. TRUTH/FALSE, *Grapefruit.* Selected items from a much longer and very funny QUESTIONNAIRE, 1966 spring.

10. BLOOD OBJECTS is a series of sculptures by Ono. The work mentioned here is: *High-Heeled Shoes (Blood Object)*, 1993, patinated bronze and red paint, 8 3/8 X 3 X 5 3/16". A photo of this work (photo: William Nettles) was printed in an article by Robert Enright, "Instructions in the Marital Arts, a Conversation with Yoko Ono", *BorderCrossings*, Volume 13, Number 1, January 1994, pp. 30-41.

11. CLOSET PIECE I, CLOSET PIECE II, appear in *Grapefruit* and are dated 1964 spring.

12. John and Yoko, from *The Wedding Album,* John Lennon/Yoko Ono, 1969. Reissued on CD by Rykodisk, 1997.

13. DANGER BOX, as described in ONO'S SALES LIST © 1965, *Grapefruit.* Bargain basement price at the time: $1,1000 —

14. SMOKE PIECE, 1964. *Grapefruit.*

15. Please see "Yoko Ono and Her Sixteen-Track Voice," by Jonathan Cott, *Rolling Stone* Magazine, March 18, 1971. Reprinted in *The Ballad of John and Yoko*, (p. 116).

16. In 1969, John and Yoko celebrated their honeymoon by staging a performance art event/press conference, "Bed-in for Peace", in Amsterdam, Toronto, and Montreal. Excellent footage can be seen in the film *John Lennon: Imagine* (1988), ready to rent at your local video stores.

17. The WAR IS OVER! campaign for peace was launched in December 1969, in twelve cities around the world. In Toronto, thirty roadside billboards went up, along with posters, handbills, and newspaper ads.

18. "Give Peace a Chance", (John Lennon/Paul McCartney) © 1969 Maclean Music/ BMI. Produced by John and Yoko (BAG), recorded in Room 1742, Montreal, Canada.

19. YELLOW TALK is part of QUESTIONNAIRE, 1966 spring, and appears in *Grapefruit*. Here, it is very slightly edited for staging purposes.

20. *Bottoms, Film No. 4*, is a black and white film by Yoko Ono created in 1967. Initially banned in Britain as obscene, *Bottoms* features 365 bare asses, in motion. Four quadrants shifting. A sound track of interviews with the potential actors accompanies the film.

21. There are excellent photos in *Yoko Ono: Arias & Objects.* It's worth noting, because his photos are so starkly beautiful, that the images of Ono in this period were all shot by Iain Macmillan.

22. *Apple,* 1966.

23. *Ceiling Painting*, 1966. From *Yoko Ono: Arias & Objects.*

24. *Painting to Hammer a Nail In.* From *Yoko Ono: Arias & Objects.*

25. Clip of John and Yoko from *Two Virgins* (film, 1968), their faces dissolving in an out, morphing, merging.

26. *Unfinished Music No. 1, Two Virgins*, Yoko Ono/John Lennon, recorded and released 1968, reissued by Tetragrammaton Records, 1997. Photos by John Lennon.

27. Please see "Yoko Ono and Her Sixteen-Track Voice," by Jonathan Cott, *Rolling Stone Magazine*, (March 18, 1971); reprinted in *The Ballad of John and Yoko*, (pp. 124-125).

28. *Eternal Time Clock*, 1965. *Yoko Ono: Arias and Objects* (p. 56).

29. "All my work is a form of wishing." Yoko Ono in conversation with Robert Enright, "Instructions in the Marital Arts, a Conversation with Yoko Ono",*BorderCrossings*, Volume 13, Number 1, January 1994 (p. 39).

30. "I thought art was a verb rather than a noun so I wanted an action quality to the experience." *ibid*

31. In addition to a still image of *Eternal Time Clock*, the perfect world would include images that pop in and out during the scene including a still of ONO in a black dress with an image of a Dada-esque clock (*Mrs. Lennon/Imagine, 1971*) and a repeat of *Bottoms: Film Number 4* (1967).

32. *Cut Piece*, as described in Grapefruit.

33. Written for the production of *Stone* at Judson Church Gallery, New York, March 1966. Reprinted in *Grapefruit*.

34. WHISPER PIECE, *Grapefruit.*

35. "Walking on Thin Ice", words and music by Yoko Ono, on *Season of Glass* (1981).

36. LINE TALK is a section of A, B, or C, part of QUESTIONNAIRE, 1966 spring, and appears in *Grapefruit*.

37. This text is from LINE PIECE, and appears in *Grapefruit*.

38. "Mind Holes", Yoko Ono.

39. This image accompanies the article by Charles McCarry, "John Rennon's Excrusive Gloupie, the Yoko Nobody Ono's", *Esquire Magazine,* December 1970.

40. "Rising", music and lyrics by Yoko Ono, composed and recorded 1994.

41. Jonah Weslak, *Watch Magazine*, Toronto, January 1996, (p. 31).

42. Opening sound byte of "No, No, No", words and music by Yoko Ono. *Season of Glass* (1981).

43. QUESTION PIECE, *Grapefruit*.

44. Film clips/images: John and Yoko waltzing (*Woman/Imagine, 1971*); walking on the beach (*Jealous Guy*, 1971); making love (*Walking on Thin Ice*); running into each other's arms (*Mrs. Lennon/Imagine, 1971*); dissolving to details of back cover image of *Life with Lions*, Yoko clearly frightened and in pain in John's arms, police all around; close-up of Yoko crying (*Mrs. Lennon/Imagine, 1971*).

45. From an interview with Ono ... *TBC* ...

46. Selected items from ONO'S SALES LIST, N.Y.C. 1965, *Grapefruit*.

47. "Yes, I'm Your Angel", by Yoko Ono, on *Double Fantasy*, recorded 1980, released 1981.

About the Author

photo by Tim Leyes

Jean Yoon is a writer, actor and theatre artist living in Toronto. She was Co-Artistic Director of Cahoots Theatre Projects (1992-1994) and is currently Seoul Babe/Artistic Director of Loud Mouth Asian Babes, a company dedicated to developing and producing "Theatre for the Dis/Oriented and Culturally Confused." Other works for the stage include "Sliding for Home & Borders", produced by LMAB in 1995, and "Spite", a one woman piece presented at Summerworks 2000.

A Selection of Our Titles in Print

A Fredericton Alphabet (John Leroux) photos, architecture, ISBN 1-896647-77-4
All the Perfect Disguises (Lorri Neilsen Glenn) poetry, 1-55391-010-9
Antimatter (Hugh Hazelton) poetry, 1-896647-98-7
Avoidance Tactics (Sky Gilbert) drama, 1-896647-50-2
Bathory (Moynan King) drama, 1-896647-36-7
Break the Silence (Denise DeMoura) poetry, 1-896647-87-1
Combustible Light (Matt Santateresa) poetry, 0-921411-97-9
Crossroads Cant (Mary Elizabeth Grace, Mark Seabrook, Shafiq, Ann Shin. Joe Blades, editor) poetry, 0-921411-48-0
Cuerpo amado/ Beloved Body (Nela Rio; Hugh Hazelton, translator) poetry, 1-896647-81-2
Dark Seasons (Georg Trakl; Robin Skelton, translator) poetry, 0-921411-22-7
Day of the Dog-tooth Violets (Christina Kilbourne) fiction, 1-896647-44-8
During Nights That Undress Other Nights/ En las noches que desvisten otras noches (Nela Rio; Elizabeth Gamble Miller, translator) poetry, 1-55391-008-7
for a cappuccino on Bloor (kath maclean) poetry, 0-921411-74-X
Great Lakes logia (Joe Blades, editor) art & writing anthology, 1-896647-70-7
Heart-Beat of Healing (Denise DeMoura) poetry, 0-921411-24-3
Heaven of Small Moments (Allan Cooper) poetry, 0-921411-79-0
Herbarium of Souls (Vladimir Tasic) short fiction, 0-921411-72-3
I Hope It Don't Rain Tonight (Phillip Igloliorti) poetry, 0-921411-57-X
Jive Talk: George Fetherling in Interviews and Documents (Joe Blades, editor), 1-896647-54-5
Mangoes on the Maple Tree (Uma Parameswaran) fiction, 1-896647-79-0
Manitoba highway map (rob mclennan) poetry, 0-921411-89-8
Paper Hotel (rob mclennan) poetry, 1-55391-004-4
Railway Station (karl wendt) poetry, 0-921411-82-0
Reader Be Thou Also Ready (Robert James) fiction, 1-896647-26-X
resume drowning (Jon Paul Fiorentino) poetry, 1-896647-94-4
Rum River (Raymond Fraser) fiction, 0-921411-61-8
Shadowy:Technicians: New Ottawa Poets (rob mclennan, editor), poetry, 0-921411-71-5
Singapore (John Palmer) drama, 1-896647-85-5
Song of the Vulgar Starling (Eric Miller) poetry, 0-921411-93-6
Speaking Through Jagged Rock (Connie Fife) poetry, 0-921411-99-5
Starting from Promise (Lorne Dufour) poetry, 1-896647-52-9
Sunset (Pablo Urbanyi; Hugh Hazelton, translator) fiction, 1-55391-014-1
Sweet Mother Prophesy (Andrew Titus) fiction, 1-55391-002-8
Tales for an Urban Sky (Alice Major) poetry, 1-896647-11-1
The Longest Winter (Julie Doiron, Ian Roy) photos, short fiction, 0-921411-95-2
This Day Full of Promise (Michael Dennis) poetry, 1-896647-48-0
The Sweet Smell of Mother's Milk-Wet Bodice (Uma Parameswaran) fiction, 1-896647-72-3
The Yoko Ono Project (Jean Yoon) drama, 1-55391-001-X
Túnel de proa verde/ Tunnel of the Green Prow (Nela Rio; Hugh Hazelton, translator) poetry, 0-921411-80-4
What Was Always Hers (Uma Parameswaran) short fiction, 1-896647-12-X

www.brokenjaw.com hosts our current catalogue, submissions guidelines, manuscript award competitions, booktrade sales representation and distribution information. Broken Jaw Press eBooks of selected titles are available from http://www.PublishingOnline.com. Directly from us, all individual orders must be prepaid. All Canadian orders must add 7% GST/HST (Canada Customs and Revenue Agency Number: 12489 7943 RT0001).

BROKEN JAW PRESS, Box 596 Stn A, Fredericton NB E3B 5A6, Canada